The European Union

Jillian Powell

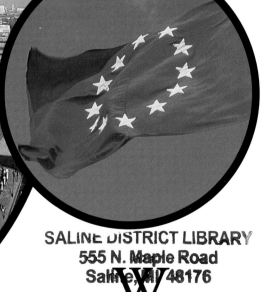

W

FRANKLIN WATTS

A Division of Grolier Publishing

NEW YORK • LONDON • HONG KONG • SYDNEY
DANBURY, CONNECTICUT

AP

Picture credits: Cover: Impact, Tony Page (main), Panos, Chris Sattlberger (top right), EU (bottom right). Inside: CCE: 20; Courtesy of Temple Bar Properties: 12 (bottom). Holt Studios: 14 (bottom), 15 (bottom) Nigel Cattlin. Impact: 3 (top and bottom), 13 W. Louvet, 17 (bottom) Simon Shepheard, 25. Popperfoto: 2 (top and center), 4, 5 (top), 7 Yves Herman, 8 (bottom) Vincent Kessler, 9 (bottom) Olivier Hoslet, 12 (top), 19 (top) Pascal Rossignol, 19 (bottom) Ian Hodgson, 22 Benoit Doppagne, 24 (top), 24 (bottom) Kai Pfaffenbach, 26 Achim Bieniek, 29 Vincent Kessler. Rex Features: 6 Martin Lee, 11 Lehtikuva/Markku, 16 (top) J. Sutton, 18 (right), 23 Tim Norman, 27. RSPB Images: 29 Andrew Hay. Still Pictures: 17 (top) Hartmut Scwarzbach, 18 (left) John Maier, 28 Jo Elms/Christian Aid. Topham 5 (bottom) AP, 9 (top), 10 Richard Laird, 14 (top), 15 (top), 16 (bottom) Barry Batchelor.

First published in 2001 by Franklin Watts

Series Editor: Anderley Moore
Designer: Simon Borrough
Picture Research: Sue Mennell
Consultant: Graham Welch, European Commission. This title was produced with the European Commission's advice, but the views expressed within do not necessarily reflect the views of the European Commission.

First American edition 2001 by
Franklin Watts
A Division of Grolier Publishing
90 Sherman Turnpike
Danbury, CT 06816

Visit Franklin Watts on the Internet at:
http://publishing.grolier.com

Catalog-in-Publication Data is available from the Library of Congress
ISBN 0-531-14620-0

GROLIER
PUBLISHING
Printed in Malaysia
© Franklin Watts 2001

After World War II (1939–45), in which 55 million people died, governments began to look for ways of building closer links among the countries of Europe to prevent further wars.

In 1951, six European countries (France, Belgium, West Germany, Luxembourg, Italy, and the Netherlands) set up the European Coal and Steel Community (ECSC). Their aim was to protect the interests of their steel and coal industries. In 1957 they joined together to form the European Economic Community (EEC) by signing the Treaty of Rome.

▼ *European leaders meet to sign the Treaty of Rome in 1957.*

EU member states and year of joining

1957
Belgium
France
Germany, West
Italy
Luxembourg
Netherlands

1973
Denmark
Ireland
United Kingdom

1981
Greece

1986
Portugal
Spain

1995
Austria
Finland
Sweden

Growth of the European Union

During the 1970s and 80s, more countries applied to join the European Community. Starting in 1979, direct elections were held for the European Parliament. This meant that Europeans could vote every five years for the Members of European Parliament (MEPs) they wanted to represent them.

In 1992, the twelve member states signed the Treaty on European Union, agreeing to work to develop the community into a political, economic, and monetary union, and, in doing so, also changing its name.

During its history, the EU has grown in size and power. Enlargement will continue as more countries in central and eastern Europe join.

▼ *Like all citizens of Europe, UK citizens hold a European-format passport.*

▲ *European Union heads of state get together in 1999 to discuss the crisis in Kosovo.*

▲ *The flag of the EU has a circle of stars representing the union of member states.*

Today, the European Union still aims to promote peace in Europe. It is also involved in trying to raise the standard of living for all EU citizens, improving trade, and spreading European wealth more evenly. The EU has its own emblem and anthem, and Europe Day is celebrated every year on May 9 in member states.

The countries that have joined the EU are known as member states. They work to improve living and working conditions, to represent Europe to the rest of the world, and to give their peoples the benefit of European rulings on citizens' rights.

All member states have democratic governments — these are governments that are elected by their people. There are now fifteen member states of the EU, mostly from western Europe, and other central and eastern European countries have applied to join.

Main Aims of the EU

- To form a closer union among European peoples
- To improve their working and living conditions
- To get rid of barriers to trade among member states
- To allow people, goods, services, and money to move freely throughout the Union

EU Citizens

The European Union has more than doubled since the Treaty of Rome was signed in 1957 — the point that marks the official beginning of the European Union. There are now about 370 million EU citizens. Anyone who is a citizen of a member state is also a citizen of the EU.

Spotlight

Each year since 1985, the Council of Ministers of Culture of the EU has chosen a "cultural capital of Europe." The city is given grants to develop culture and the arts for its people and visitors. There were nine European Cities of Culture in the year 2000: Avignon, Bergen, Bologna, Brussels, Kraków, Helsinki, Prague, Reykjavik, and Santiago de Compostella.

▲ Celebrations in Brussels, one of the nine European Cities of Culture chosen in 2000.

Spotlight

A wide range of languages is spoken in the EU. All legislation and formal and other documents are prepared in the eleven official languages of the fifteen member states. English and French are most often used for meetings. A team of interpreters translates each language at official meetings. Translated EU documents are color-coded: for example, papers in English are pink, and papers in French are blue. In the Court of Justice, a language of the case is chosen, and translation and interpretation are provided.

European citizens have the right to

- move and live anywhere within the EU
- vote and stand in local government and European Parliament elections
- be helped if in trouble when traveling in non-EU countries
- petition and appeal to the European ombudsman (the highest official)

The European Union is run by representatives from its member states. Member states alternate holding the presidency of the EU for six months. Portugal held it at the start of the year 2000.

The European Commission

One of the EU's institutions, the European Commission, has twenty commissioners selected from each country in the EU. Its main job is to make sure that the policies written down in the treaties are carried out and to defend the interests of EU citizens. The commission is based in Brussels, and its staffs work in Brussels and Luxembourg. Its president is nominated by member state governments and approved by the European Parliament. In the middle of the year 2000, Romano Prodi of Italy held the post.

▶ Romano Prodi, president of the European Commission, at a news conference in Strasbourg, France.

The Council of Ministers

The council, based in Brussels, is the highest decision-making organization within the EU and the most powerful of its institutions. There are fifteen ministers in the council. On particularly important decisions, every member must agree. Any member state, however small, can block a decision in the council.

The European Parliament

The 370 million European citizens of the EU are represented by the European Parliament. There are 626 Members of the European Parliament (MEPs), each directly elected by the people in their European Constituency (the area they represent) for five-year terms. The number of members from each member state is based on the size

▲ *The European Parliament buildings in Strasbourg.*

of its population. The parliament meets in Strasbourg, and its staff, the Secretariat, works in Luxembourg. It debates proposals from the commission and the council and watches over the work of the commission.

◀ *Members of the European Parliament (MEPs) in session.*

The multi-layered system of EU government can be loosely compared with the United States, which has a supreme national government under an elected president and many state governments and smaller units governing states, cities, and towns. This means that the balance of power is evenly distributed, and the likelihood of corruption at the top is reduced.

 Spotlight

If MEPs are concerned about any area of EU policy, they can hold question-and-answer sessions with members of the commission. In March 2000, the Agriculture Committee of the European Parliament put questions to Environment Commissioner Margot Walström. They were concerned that EU policies aimed at reducing the amount of nitrates in the environment were not taking effect. MEPs argued that there had been delays because the EU had not considered the cost to farmers.

The European Ombudsman

An ombudsman is like a watchdog. This person can receive complaints from any European citizen against any EU institution. The ombudsman investigates complaints and suggests changes or improvements in the way things are done. The European ombudsman is appointed by the parliament.

◀ The White House, in Washington, D.C., home of the president of the United States.

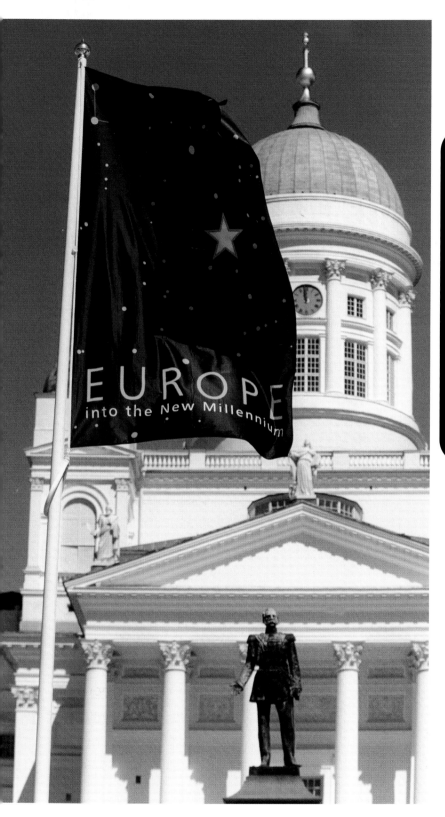

◀ *Finland's EU flag flying at the Senate Square in Helsinki. Finland held the EU presidency in 1999.*

 Spotlight

In 1992, the Committee on the Environment, Public Health, and Consumer Protection introduced an EU eco-label for environmentally friendly products. The Euro-flower was awarded to companies making "green" goods, including washing machines, laundry detergents, and lightbulbs.

The Court of Justice

The European Court of Justice is based in Luxembourg and has fifteen judges, one from each member state, helped by nine senior lawyers. The court sees that member states follow the policies set out in the treaties. It can issue penalties and fines to member states who fail to follow EU laws. Any European citizen can bring a case to the court, which has powers to overturn decisions made in or by that citizen's own country.

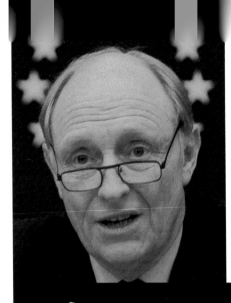

◀ *Neil Kinnock is the European commissioner for administrative reforms.*

Problem

The EU is such a large organization that many Europeans feel they do not know enough about the way it works. The commission has been criticized for poor management and dishonesty. On March 15, 1999, the European Parliament forced the entire commission to resign. The vice president of the commission, Neil Kinnock, is now in charge of finding ways to reform it.

The EU Budget

The EU receives money from its member states, who pay according to how rich they are. Income also comes from duties on goods imported from outside the EU and from a small portion of sales tax. The commission works out a draft budget, which the council and parliament consider. The European Parliament has the power to adopt or reject the budget.

The commission, the council, and parliament all consult with special committees and working parties before allocating budgets. There are about three hundred special committees covering areas such as agriculture, industry, the environment, and food safety.

▼ *Dublin's docklands in the Temple Bar area have been redeveloped as a commercial center with the help of money from the EU budget.*

When the European Community was formed, one of its main aims was to make sure there would be no more food shortages in Europe, as there had been after World War II. Agricultural policies focused on making farming more efficient and ensuring fair prices for consumers and farmers. The Common Agricultural Policy (CAP) was introduced in 1962. It set out to control amounts of food produced, give grants to farmers, and buy up goods to keep prices steady.

▼ *Large, prairie-like fields of grain crops have become a familiar part of the European landscape as a result of the Common Agricultural Policy.*

▲ *CAP policies have led to surplus crops, like these plum tomatoes grown in Italy.*

▼ *EU quotas limit the amount of milk that a dairy farm can produce each year.*

Changing Farming Methods

CAP subsidies meant that farmers received a fixed price for their produce. If the butter, grain, or wine they produced was not sold, it was bought and stored by the EU, sold, or given away. This guarantee of income meant that farmers could produce single crops rather than having to practice mixed farming. CAP grants also encouraged farmers to use intensive methods of farming. Farmers took out hedges to make fields larger, drained marshland, and used more fertilizers, pesticides, and irrigation.

Intensive farming means that more food is available all year at cheaper prices, but it also has environmental costs. Rivers and soil have been polluted with chemicals, soil has been washed away, and wildlife habitats and wetland sites have been lost. The policy of buying and storing produce to keep prices up has led to huge surpluses: grain and butter mountains and oil, milk, and wine lakes.

▲ Surplus food supplies like this "apple mountain" accumulate when countries over-produce certain foods. The EU is trying to prevent such waste from occurring.

During the 1980s, the European Community introduced milk quotas (limits placed on food production according to need) and other stabilizers to limit the amount that farmers produced. To encourage less-intensive production, farmers were compensated for taking some of their land out of production as "set aside" for five years or more.

In 1992, there were reforms to the Common Agricultural Policy. Prices for cereals and beef were reduced to keep European produce competitive on the world market. More farmers were given grants for setting aside land and planting trees.

▶ European farmers are being encouraged to use fields to grow young trees for timber to reduce over-production of crops.

 Problem

CAP reforms mean that subsidies (financial help) to European farmers have been reduced. Farmers have protested against cuts in subsidies and land being taken out of production. But some people believe that subsidies led to surpluses, waste, and high food prices that made it hard for developing countries to compete on the world market.

In 1999, further reforms were made to the Common Agricultural Policy. They set out these main aims for the future:

- To modernize farms
- To improve the safety and quality of food products
- To ensure a fair and stable income for farmers
- To protect the environment
- To create new jobs in rural areas
- To improve living and working conditions

Changing Fishing Methods

European fisheries have come under increasing pressure with the growing demand for fish, and some North Sea herring and cod fisheries have been nearly used up. The EU is laying down new guidelines for the fishing industry through 2006, to establish a balance between the growing demand for fish and the need to conserve stocks in the seas.

▲ *To conserve dwindling fish stocks, undersized fish are thrown back into the sea.*

▼ *A Spanish trawler is escorted back to Plymouth after being arrested on suspicion of illegal fishing in English waters.*

Problem

The Common Fisheries Policy set quotas for fishing vessels and limited fishing in coastal zones to try and save falling fish stocks. The policy has been criticized because it means dead fish are thrown back into the sea when quotas are used up. Some people feel that fish stocks will only be saved by reducing the number of EU fishing vessels and introducing a licensing program for fishing vessels.

5. Trade and Industry

In the **EU** today, most wealth comes from service industries such as telecommunications, banking, and tourism. There has also been an increase in light industries such as the manufacture of plastics and hi-tech machinery. Most jobs in the **EU** are in the service and manufacturing industries. Agriculture now makes up less than 8 percent of total employment.

EU policies aim to encourage trade and industry and reduce poverty. Grants are given to improve transportation and the environment in poorer areas to encourage new industry. The EU aims to reduce unemployment in all its countries to about 5 percent. In 1989, EU member states signed the Social Charter, giving European citizens certain social rights in employment, training, and the working environment.

▲ *EU transportation policies have encouraged the building of new roads to improve trade and communication. For example, it has invested in the construction of the Oresund Road Bridge linking Denmark and Sweden.*

 Spotlight

The EU introduced the Single Market in 1993 to encourage trade within the EU. The Single Market means that goods can be transported from one country to another within the EU without paying duties. For example, a car made in Germany should cost the same whether it is sold in Belgium or Italy. EU transport policies aim to encourage trade in the Single Market by establishing high-speed road and rail links across the EU. A network of motorways and high-speed rail links is planned for completion by 2010.

▲ *Passing through the Channel Tunnel, the Eurostar train offers a high-speed link between the UK and European cities.*

Problem

EU imports include raw materials such as iron ore from Brazil and food products such as bananas from the Caribbean. Multinational companies often own the companies that process, ship, and sell the goods. This means that the larger companies can control the prices, forcing poorer countries to sell at low prices to stay in business. Some people argue that the EU helps developing countries earn currency through trade, but others feel it would be better to help poorer countries develop their own trade and industry.

▲ *Bananas imported from the Caribbean are unloaded at a European port.*

◄ *Timber from the Amazon region of South America is loaded onto a ship to be transported to Europe.*

Problem

The EU's Common Agricultural Policy, which gives directives on farming practices and prices, is not always popular with European farmers. For example, in 1999 more than two thousand French farmers in tractors staged a demonstration outside the European Parliament building in Strasbourg in protest against the Agricultural Policy. In the same year, another group of angry French farmers protested the EU's low price settings by blocking busy trading routes, such as the entrance to the Eurotunnel.

▲ French farmers block a main road near the Eurotunnel entrance in protest against the European Agricultural Policy.

▲ A slaughter-house worker sprays a permanent yellow dye on the carcasses of British cattle infected by BSE to ensure that they are destroyed and cannot be sold or eaten.

Problem

After the outbreak of "Mad Cow Disease," or BSE, in the UK in the late 1980s, the EU Commission banned the export of all UK British cattle and meat products. The British government took stringent measures to combat BSE and convince the European Commission that British beef was safe. The European Commission carried out regular inspections in the UK before lifting the ban in the summer of 1999. But France went against the EU ruling and refused to accept British beef because France was still worried about its safety. As a result, the EU is taking legal action against the government of France.

▲ The European Court of Justice occupies a large modern building in Luxembourg.

The treaties made between European Union countries on different subjects form the Constitution of the European Union and the basis for all its laws.

Treaties set out aims and timetables for EU policies. The treaties must be accepted by every state that applies to join the EU. They have been revised at meetings held at Maastricht and Amsterdam and are amended when new member states join the EU. The laws based on EU treaties can overrule the laws of individual countries.

The European Commission makes proposals for new laws after consulting with special committees and working parties, which are made for discussions on subjects such as social policy or the Single Currency. These can lead to White Papers, which are practical proposals for laws. Some EU laws, including regulations and decisions, must be enforced by all member states. Others, such as directives, set out aims that member states achieve in their own way.

The commission must make sure that EU laws are followed. It has the power to take member governments to the European Court of Justice if they fail to follow EU laws.

Lobbyists

Lobbyists and pressure groups are people who work for a special cause, such as animal welfare, the environment, or human rights. They argue their cases to politicians and try to influence the making of policies and laws. Many of these groups have a base in Brussels so they can argue their case to Members of the European Parliament (MEPs) or members of the committees that advise the EU on policy.

up of government and other experts. Proposals are then debated in the European Parliament before the Council of Ministers makes decisions on new laws in consultation with parliament.

The European Commission produces Green Papers, which are documents

The European Court of Justice

The European Court of Justice is based in Luxembourg. Its main role is to see that laws based on the treaties are followed throughout the EU. If a government or company fails to follow EU laws, the court can impose fines or penalties. Any citizen of the EU can bring a case to the court. It can overrule national laws, and there is no appeal against its decisions..

Spotlight

The Bosman Ruling

In September 1995, Belgian soccer player Jean-Marc Bosman took his case to the European Court of Justice. He claimed his soccer career was ruined by the failure of his team FC Liege to honor a transfer agreement for him to move to French club Dunkerque. The court ruled in his favor, and the case changed soccer history. The Bosman ruling means that soccer clubs can no longer charge an excessive transfer fee for players wishing to switch clubs.

Spotlight

The Francovich Case

Mr. Francovich was an employee of an Italian firm that went bankrupt. A 1980 EC directive gave protection to employees following a firm's bankruptcy, but the Italian government had failed to put it into effect. The Court of Justice ruled that Mr. Francovich could claim compensation from the Italian government.

▼ Belgian soccer player Jean-Marc Bosman (center) and his lawyers hold a press conference following his hearing at the European Court of Justice.

Europe has one of the strongest economies in the world. EU economic policies aim to make the EU more effective when it trades with other parts of the world and to protect member states from the risk of sudden changes in the value of their currency.

The European Monetary System (EMS) was set up in 1979 to make exchange rates and interest rates more stable in Europe and to bring the monetary policies of member states closer together. This is to prepare them for European Monetary Union (EMU) and a Single Currency.

Exchange Rate Mechanism (ERM)

The ERM is part of the European Monetary System. Its aim is to keep exchange rates between European currencies steady. This helps European businesses because they are not at risk from their own countries' currencies suddenly getting stronger or weaker. Countries that have joined the ERM have their currencies fixed against each other and against the European Currency Unit, the euro. If they go up or down beyond the limits that have been fixed, currencies are bought or sold, or interest rates raised or lowered, to bring them back in line with the ERM.

 # Problem

The UK pound sterling joined the ERM in October 1990, but on Wednesday, September 16, 1992, frantic speculation over currencies caused by high German interest rates led to a serious fall in the value of the pound. In order to raise the pound back to acceptable levels, the treasury would have to spend large sums of money. Rather than do this, the UK left the ERM on a day that became known as Black Wednesday.

▶ *On Black Wednesday, Chancellor Norman Lamont announced that Britain was leaving the ERM.*

Thirteen of the fifteen EU member states have joined the ERM (Sweden, Denmark, and the UK have not). All countries that want to join have to show that their economies are strong enough.

The Treaty of Maastricht

The Treaty of Maastricht was signed at a meeting of the European Council in December 1991. The treaty set out three stages toward European Monetary Union (EMU) but allowed opt-outs for Denmark and the UK.

The Single Currency

The euro is the official currency of the EU. Twelve countries have adopted it by joining the ERM. This means their own currencies count as units of the euro and have a fixed exchange rate against it. In 1999, the euro began to be used as a trading currency by businesses and the international money markets. The issue of euro banknotes and coins is set for January 1, 2002. Countries within the euro zone can trade with each other without changing currencies, which means that business costs are lower and companies are not at risk from changes in the value of their country's currency.

◀ A banknote for the euro, Europe's single currency.

▼ In January 1999, the euro was launched at the European Central Bank in Frankfurt. As part of festivities to mark the occasion, thousands of people gathered around a large euro sign.

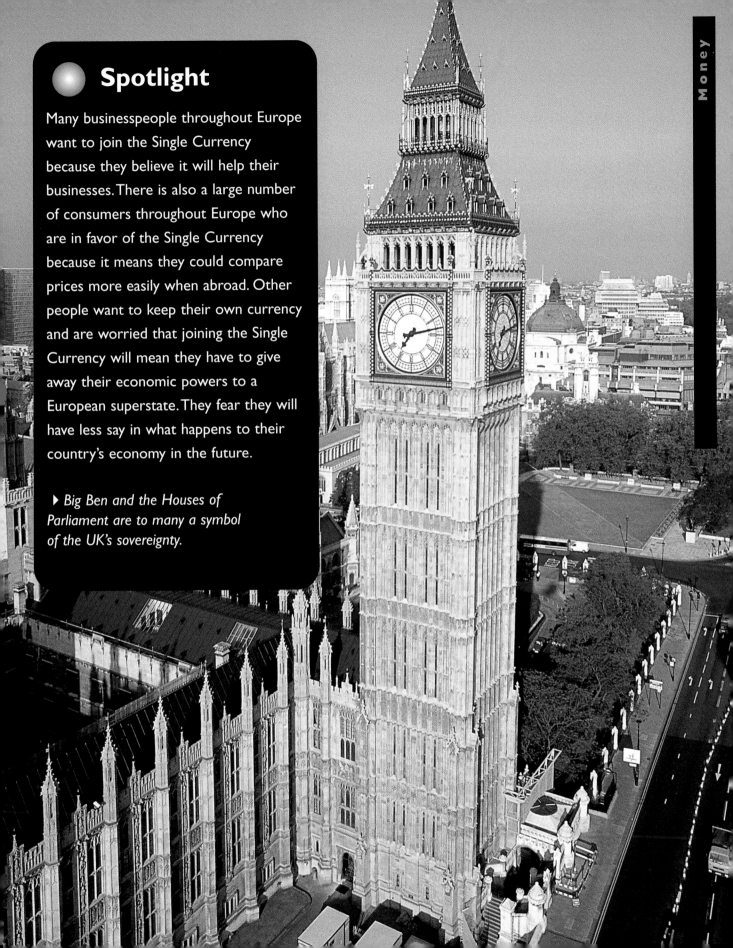

● Spotlight

Many businesspeople throughout Europe want to join the Single Currency because they believe it will help their businesses. There is also a large number of consumers throughout Europe who are in favor of the Single Currency because it means they could compare prices more easily when abroad. Other people want to keep their own currency and are worried that joining the Single Currency will mean they have to give away their economic powers to a European superstate. They fear they will have less say in what happens to their country's economy in the future.

▶ *Big Ben and the Houses of Parliament are to many a symbol of the UK's sovereignty.*

In the future, the EU could change and develop in a number of ways. Some of the issues it faces were outlined in Agenda 2000, an action program adopted by the commission on July 15, 1997.

Enlargement

As more countries in central and eastern Europe apply to join, the EU could grow. This growth is called enlargement. Negotiations began in 1998 for six countries that wish to join — Cyprus, the Czech Republic, Estonia, Hungary, Poland, and Slovenia — about the terms of their membership. Since then, seven more countries have applied for membership: Bulgaria, Latvia, Lithuania, Malta, Romania, Slovakia, and Turkey. Countries that want to join the EU must show that they have

- democratic government and political stability
- a free-market economy (in which competition in the marketplace is not restricted)
- commitment to the EU's political, economic, and monetary aims
- acceptance of EU laws

Some people want the EU to grow to include more European countries. Others believe that before it can grow bigger, it needs to make its institutions and powers stronger. Many feel that if the EU enlarges to include twenty or more countries, its institutions will need to undergo reform to represent the increased number of countries adequately.

 Spotlight

In 2000, the EU broke off relations with Austria because the government there included the ultra right-wing Freedom Party. Europeans were concerned about the Party's fascist ideas, which reminded people of Adolf Hitler and Nazi Germany. Hitler's government persecuted minority groups, such as Jews, taking away their rights and systematically destroying them. EU relations were resumed once Austria made it clear that its government still respected the rights of minorities and immigrants.

▼ *Jörg Haider, leader of the far-right Freedom Party in Austria.*

Political Union

The EU could become a political union, which means that member states would share one central European government. Some see European Monetary Union as a step toward this. Political union means transferring more powers from national governments to EU institutions.

This raises the question of sovereignty. Sovereignty means that a country's government can act independently. Some people believe that national governments should keep power, especially in areas such as defense, foreign affairs, and currency. Because of these concerns, the Treaty of Maastricht states that decisions must be made at the national, regional, or local level within a country except where they need to be made by the European Community to be effective.

▼ The civil war between Serbs and Croats made Bosnia one of the most troubled areas of Europe and a major cause for concern to the EU.

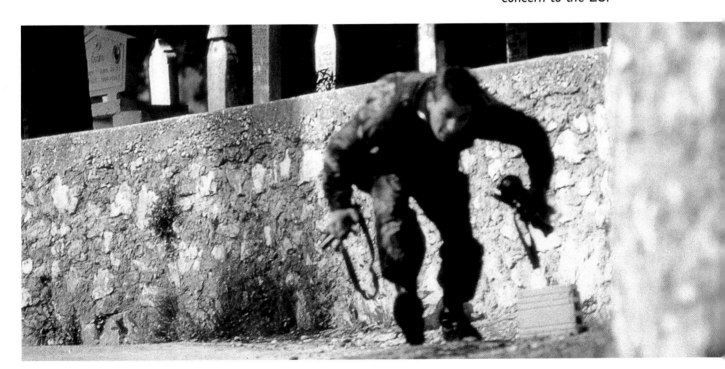

Peace in Europe

Since World War II, the threat to peace in Europe has come from disputes between groups of people of different races or religions, such as those in Bosnia-Herzegovina and Kosovo in the former Yugoslavia, and from groups who want to break away from national governments and rule themselves.

The EU is trying to reduce trouble in central and eastern Europe by investing in efforts to modernize agriculture and industry.

- The EU has spent about 1.2 billion euros helping the economies of central and eastern Europe.
- The EU is the world's largest donor of food aid to developing countries.
- The EU has spent 397 million euros on education, training, and youth projects.

In global terms, the EU has become a strong economic unit, but it does not represent a political force yet. Member states are working together to develop the Western European Union (WEU) as the defense arm of the EU. WEU members agree to make military forces available to defend European countries to help in peacekeeping or rescue tasks.

▼ The EU sends food and hygiene packages to areas such as Bosnia that are suffering as a result of war or natural disasters.

Wildlife Preservation

The EU does not concern itself merely with the interests of its citizens. As problems facing the environment become ever more pressing, the EU is also involved in wildlife protection initiatives. For example, the Royal Society for the Protection of Birds (RSPB) in the UK works with similar organizations within the European Union to monitor the numbers and safe passage of birds crossing the continent during migration.

▶ *A young bittern is ringed for an RSPB project funded by the EU to monitor the birds' migration.*

Future Citizens

The EU runs educational and training programs to improve opportunities for young people and to encourage travel and exchanges between European member states. The Tempus Program organizes exchanges between young people from the EU and the countries of central and eastern Europe, and Socrates funds courses in schools, universities, and language centers. Youth for Europe III helps young people join local training projects. Today's children and young people are the future citizens of Europe. They will help shape the EU in a fast-changing world.

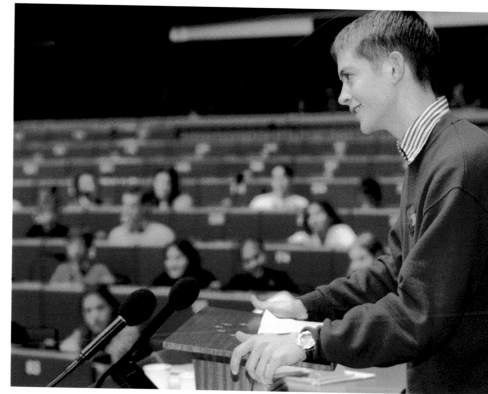

▶ *A Swedish student addresses students from other member states during a Euroschool day at the European Parliament in Strasbourg.*

budget	the amount of income and spending for a year
citizen	a member of a city, town, or country or larger community
constitution	the written document of a political entity, such as the EU or a state, which specifies the principles and goals on which it is founded
currency	coins and notes used as money
duties	amounts of money paid as tax to a government
enlargement	the word used to describe the EU's growing to include more member states
euro	the official currency of the EU
European Commission	the body of EU representatives that plans and manages policy and proposes new legislation
European Council	the supreme decision-making body of the EU
European Parliament	the elected assembly of MEPs
fisheries	areas of coastal waters and seas where fish are caught
free-market economy	an economy in which prices are fixed by competition
Green Paper	an EU document containing information to encourage debate on an issue
lobbyists	people who campaign for a cause, such as animal welfare or the environment

ombudsman	a watchdog — someone who looks into complaints
quota	the amount or share allowed
referendum	when the people of a country vote to make a decision
single market	trade between EU member states without the payment of duties
subsidy	a grant of money made to boost trade or development
treaty	a formal agreement made and signed by state governments
veto	the right to block a decision
WEU	the Western European Union — an organization set up to encourage cooperation between European countries on defense and security matters
White Paper	an EU document containing practical proposals for action on an issue

European Parliament UK Office
2 Queen Anne's Gate
London
SW1H 9AA

**Office for the Official Publications of
the European Communities**
European Commission
2 rue Mercier
2985 Luxembourg

European Information Centers (EICs) can be found
in most member states of the European Union.
The address given here is for the London branch.

Euro Info Center
London Chamber of Commerce and Industry
33 Queen Street
London EC4R JAP

www.europa.eu.int
comprehensive website for the EU, with links to
other sites

www.euroguide.org
an A to Z guide on the EU on the Internet

www.eurunion.org/profile/home.htm
a guide to the EU giving facts and figures compared
with the United States

www.europa.eu.int/euro
a guide to the euro currency

www.cec.org.uk
web site for the European Commission
Representation in London

www.ecu-notes.org
an A to Z of EU terms

www. eia.org.uk
web site for the European Information Assocation

www.europa.eu.int/scadplus
glossary of key issues and policies